PERSISTENT PRAYER

ANGELS AND DEMONS AT WORK

Colette Toach

www.ami-bookshop.com

Persistent Prayer – Angels and Demons at Work

ISBN-13: 978-1-62664-220-1

Other formats of this book:
eBook ISBN: 978-1-62664-222-5
Kindle ISBN: 978-1-62664-221-8

Copyright © 2020 by Apostolic Movement International, LLC
All rights reserved
5663 Balboa Ave #416,
San Diego,
California 92111,
United States of America

1st Printing April 2020

Published by **Apostolic Movement International, LLC**
E-mail Address: admin@ami-bookshop.com
Web Address: www.ami-bookshop.com

All rights reserved under International Copyright Law.
Contents may not be reproduced in whole or in part in any form without the express written consent of the publisher.

Unless specified, all Scripture references taken from the New King James Version®. Copyright © 1982 by Thomas Nelson. Used by permission. All rights reserved.

Contents

CHAPTER 01 Prayer: A Portal to Heaven 7
   Defining Prayer 8

CHAPTER 02 How Prayer Works 17
   Prayer – Your Spiritual Connection 21
   Hindered Prayer – Spiritual Warfare 21

CHAPTER 03 Angels at Work 27
   God Has Spoken 28
   Examples of Angels in Action 31

CHAPTER 04 Persistent Prayer 35
   Step 1: Conversation – Making the Connection 35
   Step 2: Decree – Forming a Bridge 39
   Step 3: Persistence – Downloading Your Answers .. 43

CHAPTER 05 Enter - Intercession 49
   Knowing God's Will 54
   The Five Rule Checklist 57

CHAPTER 06 We Are at WAR! 59
   A Word to the Prophets 60
   Faith Always Works 61
   Prayer Vs. Warfare 63
   First Things First – Is That Your Promised Land? 65
   Balancing Prayer and Warfare 66

CHAPTER 07 Internal Warfare 67
Sign of Warfare: God's Voice Is Not Clear 69
Getting in Line With the Message - The Garden of Gethsemane 73
Fruit of Internal Warfare 77
Bringing Your Soul Into Line 80
Fruit of Internal Warfare Summary 80

CHAPTER 08 Prophetic Warfare 81
Come on Prophets… Are You Ready for This? 83
War Against Principalities 91
Fruit of Prophetic Warfare Summary 93

CHAPTER 09 Making It Practical 95
1. Internal Warfare – Your Garden of Gethsemane 95
2. Now, Pray the Vision Through 97
3. Get Revelation! 101
4. Rebuke the Enemy 103
5. Call Circumstances Into Line 104
6. Prophesy God's Will Into the Earth! 106
Making it Practical Summary 109

Bulldozing Project 111
Bulldozing Project 111
Report Submission 114

About the Author 115
Reach Out! 116

Recommendations by the Author 117
  Prophetic Warrior 117
  How to Hear the Voice of God 117
  Strategies of War 118
  Earn a Diploma That Truly Validates Your Call 118
Contact Information 121

CHAPTER

01 Prayer: A Portal to Heaven

We are in a modern age where how we talk to one another has changed. We now have "text speak" and "chat speak". Even my five-year-old son, as he plays his games, is so much more a part of this modern world than I ever was at his age. He has a certain way of expressing himself that always gives me a good laugh.

He is very familiar with the concept of playing games on his iPad. Thank the Lord for the iPad! When we are doing a lot of traveling and we are sitting in one place for hours, it has been my lifesaver to help keep him entertained while I do what I need to do.

He got so familiar with the concept of downloading and playing games that when I did his math with him and asked him to write down the answer, he said to me, "Mommy, wait. It is busy downloading."

That is when I started to realize how much of a modern world we live in. He is not "thinking" anymore. He is "downloading". He is taking the answer from his mind and downloading it onto his page, where it will suddenly manifest itself in written form.

We do not send letters to each other anymore. We send emails. When my daughters were younger and I said to them, "I need to send someone a letter."

They replied, "Mom, are you going to email them?"

"No. This is an actual written letter that you put into an envelope and send across the country."

They could not comprehend what I was talking about. They thought, "Why would you want to do that? Why don't you just send them an email?"

Defining Prayer

With this concept in mind, I am going to use these illustrations for the message that I want to share with you in this chapter. We are all familiar with these modern terms and I thought that they would make a beautiful picture of what prayer is really about.

However, before I go into this, here are the three key passages that I want you to study for yourself:

> ### *Genesis 28:12-13*
>
> *Then he dreamed, and behold, a ladder was set up on the earth, and its top reached to heaven; and there the angels of God were ascending and descending on it.*
>
> *13 And behold, the LORD stood above it and said: "I am the LORD God of Abraham your father and the God of Isaac; the land on which you lie I will give to you and your descendants.*
>
> ### *Revelation 8:3-5*
>
> *Then another angel, having a golden censer, came and stood at the altar. He was given much incense, that he should offer it with the prayers of all the saints upon the golden altar which was before the throne.*

4 And the smoke of the incense, with the prayers of the saints, ascended before God from the angel's hand.
5 Then the angel took the censer, filled it with fire from the altar, and threw it to the earth. And there were noises, thunderings, lightnings, and an earthquake.

Luke 11:2

So He said to them, "When you pray, say:
Our Father in heaven,
Hallowed be Your name.
Your kingdom come.
Your will be done
On earth as it is in heaven.

What Prayer Is

Prayer, simply put, is words that go up to the Lord and then are downloaded back to earth. Prayer is a communication of the spirit. These three passages that I just shared with you are key to understanding what prayer is, how it works, and how you can begin to get answers to your prayers.

I am going to show you that there is a lot more to prayer than you realize. When you understand the power that there is in prayer, you will see that prayer is a lot more than just a bunch of words.

> PRAYER IS TAKING HOLD OF THE REALM OF THE SPIRIT AND CAUSING THAT WHICH IS MANIFEST IN HEAVEN, TO BE MANIFEST ON EARTH.

This can take on many forms.

It may take on the form of spiritual warfare to remove satan's influence in this earth. It may be to cause something to come to pass that God has promised you, or it could be simply to take the burdens that you have been carrying and putting them aside once and for all.

Prayer is a portal to the heavenly realm. Everyone is looking for the shortcut into the realm of the spirit, to see angels and demons, and to understand the nature of God. The secret and doorway to all of these things is prayer.

It is the one way that we touch, not the knowledge of God, but the spirit of God. God is spirit. That is why prayer is essential to the life of every believer. When we touch God in the realm of the spirit - guess what happens? God touches us back.

When God touches us back, things start to happen in this earth. I am going to teach you how you should be approaching God in prayer, how you should be following through with prayer, and how to bring about results and answers to your prayer.

Every single one of us has a need, a request, to make of the Lord. Some of them are spiritual and some are temporal. Some are very personal.

Each one of us have different needs at different levels. The first question that you ask yourself is, "Is God hearing my prayer?"

I am here to tell you that this is the easiest part of prayer. Trust me, if God can even hear the prayer of a sinner, He

"He knows the desire of my heart."

I am sure that He knows the desire of your heart, but did you open up your mouth to communicate your heart to Him?

2. Prayer Allows You to Hear What God Is Saying

Once you have made that spiritual connection, you are able to start downloading. You can then hear what God has to say back to you.

When you open your heart to the Lord, you focus your eyes on Him. By doing this, you cut out the noise around you and in that moment, you put yourself in a position to listen.

Our thoughts can easily be distracted. Try to do something for me. Talk to someone out loud and try to do a simple math calculation in your mind at the same time.

It's hard, if not impossible! No, if you want the person to understand what you are saying, you find that all of your thought is going towards what you are saying. This puts you in a position to see that person and then hear their response!

> BY PRAYING OUT LOUD, YOU MAKE A CONNECTION AND THEN POSITION YOURSELF TO HEAR!

Then, when you start hearing what God is saying back to you, then you are able to release God's will into the earth.

3. Prayer Releases God's Will Into the Earth

If you want to start seeing things happen in your life, you need to start with point one. You need to make the connection first, before you can start causing things to come to pass.

Sometimes, especially at the level of experience in ministry that we operate in with the fivefold ministry, we want to move onto the meat. We want to dig into the heavier principles of prayer and intercession, but we tend to forget that we just need to begin by making a connection first.

I refreshed my mind on the subject of prayer in the Word. You will be amazed to see how many times prayer is mentioned. There are hundreds of scriptures on the word "prayer". God was not messing around. He was not giving a subtle hint as to how we might reach Him.

He made it quite clear - until you start to pray, you don't even start to connect to Him. Once connection is made, you can begin hearing Him answer. Finally, once you receive your direction, you have the authority and wisdom to release His will into this earth.

4. Prayer Blocks the Enemy

When you start releasing His will, you block the enemy from your life. You start taking ground and overcoming. You are not going to overcome until you make the connection. I have not even touched on the topic of spiritual warfare yet.

The greatest power we have as believers is to release the will of God into this earth. For as His will is released, we counter the plan the enemy had in mind. Prayer undoes the plan of the enemy! Powerful, isn't it?

5. Prayer Conforms the Natural to the Spiritual

This point is the most exciting. In other words, what is loosed in heaven is loosed in earth. What is bound in heaven, is bound in earth.

Whatever God is loosing and binding in the heavens, whatever His plan is in the heavens, when you pray, you cause the natural to be conformed to the spiritual.

That is what Matthew 16:19 is talking about. These are the keys that God has given to us as believers. We have the key of authority to use prayer to conform our natural lives to what God has set in place in heaven.

If God, in heaven, said to you, "Yes, I have given you a spouse. Yes, I have given you a ministry. Yes, I have provided your need", then imagine this beautiful program that has been designed just for you, in heaven.

What you need to do now is to download it to the natural so that you can use it in this natural world. That is what prayer does. It causes you to take the promises, the reality of heaven, the reality of God's blessing, and bring that to earth and make it a reality in your everyday walk with Him.

> PRAYER TAKES THE REALITY OF HEAVEN AND CAUSES THAT REALITY TO BE MANIFEST ON EARTH

Prayer is so much more than...

"Oh Lord, bless me."

"Oh Lord, make my problems go away."

Prayer is more than a Christian obligation.

We as a Church, have forgotten that there is power in prayer.

We have forgotten the power of its simplicity and its capacity to draw us closer to Jesus. We must return to taking time to talk! To communicate with our Father. Only then, will we be given the eyes to know the next step He is telling us to take.

CHAPTER

02 How Prayer Works

> *Isaiah 55:11*
>
> *So shall My word be that goes forth from My mouth; it shall not return to Me void, but it shall accomplish what I please, and it shall prosper in the thing for which I sent it.*

Do you know why prayer causes things that are in heaven to come to pass on this earth? It is because words contain power. Where is the Holy Spirit residing right now?

You are the temple of the Holy Spirit. Is He not dwelling within you? So, when you speak and when you act, when you do something, what is inside of you will come out.

The Word says, "Out of the abundance of the heart, the mouth speaks." (Matt 12:34)

In other words, your words and your actions carry power. As I spoke to the Lord concerning this teaching, He reminded me of the teaching that I taught called *The Law of Obedience*.

He said, "I taught you in this teaching that you come to me in prayer and supplication and then I speak back to you and I give you direction."

I say to you, "Colette, you need to take this step and deal with this blockage in your life."

However, do you know that the change only takes place when I obey the instructions that God has given to me? I actually have to get up and do what God has told me to do, to see results.

God says to you, "My child, I have given you this promise. I need you to go here, knock on this door, and follow these instructions."

The change only comes when you take action. It is your very action that releases the promise to come to pass.

> PRAYER HOLDS POWER BECAUSE IT CONTAINS BOTH WORDS AND ACTION.

You are not just speaking words when you pray. You are releasing a spiritual force into this earth. When you pray according to the will of God, according to Isaiah, that word will never ever return void, but it will accomplish that for which it was sent.

The question that you need to ask yourself is, "Am I sending the word out?"

Why were Balaam's words so dangerous to the children of Israel? It was to the point where God even made his donkey speak. Have you ever wondered why it was such a big deal?

Balaam was going to stand up on behalf of the king and for a certain fee, he was going to curse the children of Israel. God would not have it. Balaam stood there getting ready to speak satan's words and instead, the Holy Spirit came upon him, causing him to speak the words of Almighty God instead.

Why was that such a big deal? Who cares what one little prophet says? What difference can one man's words make? It could have had such an impact that God had to send an angel to set things right.

It could have brought so much change that God had to come upon Balaam again and again and twist his arm to speak His words, instead of satan's words. Balaam, even in his sin, deception, and the fact that he was a false prophet, had power in his words.

Every human being has power in their words because every human being has a spirit. A dog barks. Short of being terribly annoying that bark does not release the plan of God into this earth.

His barks and sounds do not carry power. However, the spirit of man does. Why? It is because we have been made in the image of God. If you are a human being, God has breathed life into you.

Words Carry Power

You have a spirit and you have the potential to tap into the realm of the spirit. If we as simple human beings have power in our words, how much more power do we have when the words that we are speaking are further empowered by the direction of the Holy Spirit?

That is the power of prayer. If you read through the books of Ezekiel, Isaiah, and Micah, you will see that their words came to pass. Why is this? It is because their words carried power.

When they started speaking, things started happening. Hebrews 11:7 tells us that when Noah built the ark, it was the building of that ark that condemned the world. If Noah would not have built the ark, the rains would not have come.

Actions of Obedience Carry Power

It was the fact that he took action, according to what God said. That very action, released a power that caused God's plan in heaven, to be downloaded and manifest in the earth.

If Noah had that in the Old Testament and had just a portion of what we have today, how much more authority and power do we have? We contain the fullness of the Godhead dwelling within our spirits to call those things that are not as though they were.

What is bound in heaven is bound in earth – namely every demon of darkness, poverty, sickness, fear, guilt, and every last spirit of infirmity.

We can cause those things that are in heaven, which is the blessing of God, to be loosed. We can bring to pass the promises to be above and not beneath, the head and not the tail, to walk out the blessing that God has given us as an inheritance.

Prayer – Your Spiritual Connection

We have that power, but are we using the power that God has given us? It is the power of prayer that makes it all happen. It is your spiritual connection.

> PRAYER IS YOUR PORTAL THAT WILL MAKE WHAT IS IN GOD'S MIND A REALITY IN YOUR LIFE.

Hindered Prayer – Spiritual Warfare

Now, there are some things that hinders our prayers. Just because we start praying does not make everything smooth sailing. Something happens when you make a connection to the realm of the spirit. There is a force of good and a force of evil.

Daniel 10:12-13

Then he said to me, "Do not fear, Daniel, for from the first day that you set your heart to understand, and to humble yourself before your God, your words were heard; and I have come because of your words. 13 But the prince of the kingdom of Persia withstood me twenty-one days; and behold, Michael, one of the chief princes, came to help me, for I had been left alone there with the kings of Persia.

You see, just like we, believers, can make a spiritual connection and give God license in this earth, satan has a few of his own messengers as well who want to stop that blessing from being downloaded.

He would like to disconnect your broadband. He would like to make it lag, slow down and reroute it, so that those answers do not manifest in your life. This is what we call spiritual warfare.

I will go deeper into the subject of spiritual warfare further along in this book, but realize that before you start engaging demons, the greatest way to overcome spiritual warfare is through prayer. The Word says, "We wrestle not against flesh and blood, but against principalities…" (Eph 6:12)

Until you know how to see results to prayer, your spiritual warfare will be impotent.

To Wrestle in Prayer

I want to draw your mind to the word "wrestle". We wrestle. It is not a boxing match, a race, or even high jump. It is wrestling. Wrestling is a full contact sport! Your opponent grabs you and you grab your opponent. You shift your body weight until such a time when you can pin them down and keep them down.

If you show a moment of weakness or your foot slips, your opponent will rise up and in turn, pin you down. That is what it means to wrestle with prayer. That is why prayer is not just a walk in the park.

It is not just something that you do every morning as a "Thank you Lord for a good day… Amen." Prayer causes you to engage in the realm of the spirit to not only release and manifest God's plan in this earth, but to also wrestle continually against the work of the enemy. Prayer is meant brother and resolve your conflict first." Then, you can go and pray. (Matt 5:23-24)

Why is this?

> YOUR BROTHER HAS THE POWER TO HINDER YOUR PRAYER AND YOU HAVE THE POWER TO HINDER YOUR BROTHER'S PRAYER.

If there is bitterness, anger or anything that connects you to your brother's sin, or vice versa, you are hindering each other's prayer.

Will your prayer eventually go through? Absolutely! With faith, it is possible. You can keep praying and praying and even on a slow connection, an old dial-up connection, you can eventually download that program… over the course of a year!

However, I am so into Fiber and DSL because I can do the same thing in seconds. Get me a high-speed connection anytime and I am downloading instantly.

Sure, with persistence and faith, you can move away those hindrances. However, you could also just take the hindrances out of the way, get a faster connection, and get your prayer answered. It is really up to you.

3. People Praying Against Us Hinders Our Prayer

People praying against you, especially those with spiritual authority, hinder your prayer as well. It does not make your prayer null and void, take your prayer away, or remove your faith, but it certainly is a hindrance.

This is spiritual warfare. Satan cannot trip you up or remove your footing, unless he has been given license to do so. He will take that license* from:

- Your personal sin
- Partaking in the sins of others
- Getting angry, or allowing someone else's anger into your life
- Others who are praying against you and your heart is open to that person to receive
- Unforgiveness and coming under false obligation

The more your heart is open to those people, the more those opposing prayers will hinder you. This is spiritual warfare. That is why we have to get on our faces before the Lord, get ourselves right and then fight back.

* These are just a few ways that the enemy gains license. For a full teaching on this, please refer to the book, *Strategies of War*

CHAPTER 03 ANGELS AT WORK

> ***Genesis 28:12-13***
>
> *Then he dreamed, and behold, a ladder was set up on the earth, and its top reached to heaven; and there the angels of God were ascending and descending on it.*
>
> *13 And behold, the LORD stood above it and said: "I am the LORD God of Abraham your father and the God of Isaac; the land on which you lie I will give to you and your descendants.*

As I already shared, we are in a wrestling match. So yes, we have to wrestle, but there is yet something else that gives us the upper hand. Let us not overlook the work of angels.

Let's bring up one of the passages I asked you to study in Chapter 1, namely Genesis 28:12-14. Here we see mention of what we know as Jacob's ladder.

Jacob was asleep and he had this dream of a ladder that was stretched from earth to heaven. What did he see on that ladder? He saw angels ascending and descending with God at the top of that ladder.

God sends forth a decree, "I am giving you the land. This land, Jacob, I have given to you."

Where was God in this vision? He was at the top of the ladder, standing in heaven. Jacob was standing on earth. There was a ladder, a spiritual connection between earth and heaven, and angels were moving up and down the ladder.

God Has Spoken

They were downloading God's plan from heaven to earth. God did not give His decree standing on the earth. God did not give His decree running up and down the ladder. God stood at the top of the ladder, sent forth the decree, and the angels ran up and down and caused that decree to come to pass.

Look at the beautiful scripture in Revelation 8 of an angel with incense, representing the prayers of all the saints. I love the part where it says that he took the censer and filled it with the fire of the altar. Then, he cast it into the earth.

Can you see this picture? We have all the prayers of the saints going up to heaven and filling the censer. Then the angel comes before the Lord in the Throne Room and says, "Here are all the prayers of the saints."

God empowers those prayers, adds fire to those prayers, and multiplies those prayers.

> THE LORD TAKES THE POWER IN YOUR HUMAN SPIRIT AND ADDS THE FIRE AND POWER OF THE HOLY SPIRIT. HE THEN TAKES ALL THAT AND SENDS IT BACK TO EARTH.

In Revelation 8:5, it says that what followed were voices, thunderings and lightnings and an earthquake. I get so excited when I read that. Let's start causing earthquakes and thunder and lightning in this earth!

Let's get those prayers up to heaven because when we do that in faith, God does not leave them there. He adds His fire and power to them and then sends them right on back down to earth!

Ministering Spirits

The angels are the ones who bring it down. They are the ministering spirits, the ones that do the will of God. They are there to minister to the saints, the righteous ones of God. That means you and me - the ones who are the heirs of salvation.

They are the ones that do the Lord's bidding. They download the things that are in heaven and cause them to be manifest in this earth. It is for them to bring God's word to pass. They make it happen.

It is like this: your prayer goes up to heaven, God hears your prayer and He says, "That is the fervent prayer of a righteous man and it avails much. To that prayer, I say 'Yes!' because he is praying according to my Word."

Other times, the prayer goes up to heaven and He says, "They are not praying according to my Word, they are praying in the flesh. The answer is no." Then, the connection is dropped.

Pray according to the will of God and according to His promise.

Angels at Work

So, you pray, you seek Him, and He hears your prayer. Then, He sends forth a decree from the top of that ladder and He says, "Yes and Amen! Whatever you bind on earth is bound in heaven and whatever you loose on earth is loosed in heaven."

He gives you authority because He has given you His promise and He says, "Yes!"

The promise comes forth, you pray to the Lord, journal, seek Him, come into His presence and then the answer comes:

"Yes, I have given you this land."

Did Jacob wake up with the deed in his hand? He had a bit of a journey to go through. Fortunately for Jacob, he was not alone. He had angels helping him to do the job. They were going between heaven and earth, downloading and causing the plan that was in heaven to come to pass.

That is how the angels work on your behalf as well. You send forth your prayer. God answers your prayer. God gives you the promise and then the angels cause that promise to come to pass.

> ANGELS WILL ONLY RESPOND TO THE WORD OF GOD.

They recognize the sound of the King. It is like a dog whistle. A dog whistle is a whistle that has such a high frequency that only dogs can hear it.

You blow this whistle and humans cannot hear it, but the dogs will start going crazy in the backyard. Angels have a bit of a "dog whistle" kind of hearing.

When they hear the word of God, their ears prick up. They say, "There goes the whistle, guys. It is time to get to work. Let's get down that ladder and let's start downloading."

However, when you come with your duck call, their ears become deaf. They do not hear your prayers. Things do not happen. When you get an answer from God, God sends the angels in reply.

> YOU PRAY, THE LORD HEARS YOUR PRAYERS, AND THEN HE SENDS THE ANGELS TO BRING IT TO PASS.

Examples of Angels in Action

Luke 1:13

But the angel said to him, "Do not be afraid, Zacharias, for your prayer is heard; and your wife Elizabeth will bear you a son, and you shall call his name John.

The angel said, "Because your prayer was heard, your wife Elizabeth will bear a son." Did you ever wonder why Elizabeth and Zacharias were chosen? There were so many in the house of Aaron that could have been picked.

Why Zacharias? I am sure that he was not the only righteous one or the only one that burned incense. They all had a turn. Why him?

Well, it turns out that he was the one that was praying. He was praying to the Lord, "Give us a son."

Then, the angel came to him and said, "Your prayer was heard." As a result, there was an angel to confirm that prayer. Then, along came John the Baptist.

When did Moses have his burning bush experience where the angel of the Lord spoke out of the bush? To paraphrase Exodus 3:7, "My people have cried out to me and their cry brought forth a response!" God's response came in the form of a burning bush.

Hagar was lying in the wilderness weeping over her son, crying out to God. The angel comes and says, "What is your request?" Then, he gives her the answer that she was looking for.

It was only when she prayed, touched God, and made that spiritual connection that the angel appeared. Cornelius - what was he doing at his time of visitation? Was he having tea? He was praying!

The Scriptures say that the angel came and said, "God has heard your prayers and He sent me."

Then, there was Daniel who was praying and the angel came to him and said, "God heard your words and He sent me."

Let's not forget Peter, who was having a nap in prison. I am guessing that he had such a busy ministry time that he would have slept anywhere. What happened while he was in prison?

The book of Acts says that the church prayed without ceasing. What happened when the church prayed without ceasing?

Peter literally got kicked in the side by the angel because he was napping so deeply. The angel said, "Come on! It is time to leave! People have been praying. It went up to heaven. God heard you. I am here. Let's go."

Just start by talking to Him. I do not care if you are an unbeliever, if you have only been born again for a day, or if you have been born again all your life. Start talking to God. Make a connection.

Until you make a connection, you are not going to follow the rest of these steps and you are not going to see answers for anything.

Keep Your Connection Open

Is it any surprise then that the Scripture says to pray without ceasing? Keep the connection open. Keep Him as part of your life. This is the first step to entering into a face-to-face relationship with Jesus.

I teach the prophets in our school this really cool project called "Practicing His Presence". I say, "Whenever you go through the day and in whatever you are doing, imagine Jesus right there with you."

If you are going down to the local coffee shop say, "Hey Jesus, I really love this latte."

Imagine Him sitting there with you in the coffee shop.

If you are busy doing your work, imagine Him sitting across the way and say, "That was a tough problem. Lord, give me wisdom. Help me out."

The point is to be aware of Him and to be in touch with Him. It does not mean that you need to be deep and get revelation all the time. It is just practicing His presence because He is already there with you and you just need an awareness of Him.

> YOU CAN CREATE AN ONGOING AWARENESS OF GOD BY SIMPLY PRACTICING HIS PRESENCE AND KEEPING THE CONVERSATION GOING.

When you do that, something amazing will happen. God will start talking back.

You may start out just feeling peace. You will go to Him with all of your anxiety, with your giving of thanks, and your requests, and then you will feel deep peace settle over you.

You may also be journaling and spewing out all the things that are frustrating you and then God might come back with a word of encouragement. He might even send someone to you with a word of encouragement.

He will say, "My child, I have been there all along. I have seen you go through these hard times. Hang in there. I will see you through to the end. Did I not say it, and will I not do it? I will make it good. I will bring the promise to pass.

This land is your land. I have promised you this land and I am not going to retract my promise from you."

He will say things like, "You need to put away that bitterness in your heart. You need to take that new step and go for that job interview."

You will start hearing Him talk back. When you start hearing Him talk back, your journey begins. When God talks back to you, He is revealing to you the plan and pattern that is in heaven.

You see, you make the connection. You get yourself hooked up to the heavenly realm. You pour out that prayer and supplication and everything that is in your spirit to the Lord. Then the Lord says, "Yes and Amen! This is my plan. This is my purpose."

It Starts Here - The Promise Is Given

Until action is taken, nothing will happen. Jacob was given an incredible promise, but he had to work for that promise. He had to go to a new land and get married. He had to work for Laban, and he had to continue to hear from God.

God gave him dream after dream of how to breed goats and when to leave Laban and go back to his father. He followed through again and again, confirming, reiterating and establishing the promise that had been given to him so many years prior.

He did not relent. The journey began when the promise came, but from there the promise had to be declared into the earth.

Step 2: Decree – Forming a Bridge

When you decree that promise into the earth, the ladder is formed and put in place. What went up as incense becomes established as a bridge between heaven and earth and the process can now begin.

Think about that. How many times has God given you a promise and you said, "Wow! That is nice."

Did you do something with it? Did you decree it into the earth? Did you establish it?

"Yes, I did."

Good. You have only completed steps one and two. You have left out step three, which I will be getting to soon.

Authority Matters - Condition of the Bridge

Authority matters. Let's say you have a need and have been seeking the Lord about something. So you journal, pray, and hear Him in the still, small voice. Perhaps you get the answer in your journal or maybe He even sends you a prophet.

It could even be that your neighbor gets a word for you. There are many ways to hear the voice of God. However, you heard from Him, you know that this is God's promise to you.

To you, this is like the dream Jacob had. That decree needs to be sent forth into the earth. It is that very decree that will establish that bridge. It is like the angel adding fire to the prayers. It literally conceives the promise.

Depending on whether or not that is done with authority will determine whether or not a bridge is formed in the first place. If it is just a good idea, it will fall to the ground and have no effect.

> WHAT KIND OF BRIDGE ARE YOU FORMING BETWEEN HEAVEN AND EARTH? THAT BRIDGE IS FORMED WITH THE POWER OF DECREE TO DECLARE THE PROMISES OF GOD.

John 19:11

Jesus answered, you would have no authority against me whatsoever, unless it were given to you from a higher authority: therefore whoever handed me over to you has the greater sin.

Authority matters. God is the ultimate authority and He is the only one who can delegate authority. As a human being, we have a little bit of His authority.

The Lord gave His authority to Adam in this earth. He needed to tend and keep the earth and even now man continues to do that. Man has authority and dominion over the earth.

We pull oil from the ground and fruit from the trees. We rule the earth and the animals. That has always been God's order. As a believer, you have more authority because you have the Holy Spirit dwelling inside of you.

When an unbeliever speaks a word into the earth, yes, they will get results. Have you ever wondered how unbelievers get results when they push through saying, "I will get through this? I will accomplish this. The power of positive thinking. What a man thinks, so is he."

They say it and say it and it eventually comes to pass. How so? It is because they have a bit of God's authority in them. God gave that authority to man to begin with. However, when you get born again, you have a greater level of authority because you have the Holy Spirit inside of you.

You have the keys of the kingdom that can declare, "This door will be opened and that door will be closed." If this applies to a born-again believer, how much more to someone who holds a fivefold ministry office and given more authority?

> *2 Corinthians 13:10*
>
> *Therefore I write these things being absent, lest being present I should use sharpness, according to the power which the Lord has given me to edification, and not to destruction.*

Apostle Paul is speaking specifically of his apostleship here. He said that he received authority directly from the Lord. He did not say, "Authority given to us." He did not use the word "us" as if he were speaking to all believers.

He said, "me". As an apostle, he was given authority. This is mentioned more than once in the Scriptures regarding the elders and leaders that were given authority.

Prophets and Decree

The size of your bridge will depend on your level of authority. So yes, if you have a prophet decreeing, things will happen faster. Hence, the power of intercession.

That is why we need leaders in the Church to stand up and decree and release God's blessing over the lives of His people. That decree establishes the bridge.

The authority with which you speak is going to determine whether it is a tiny bridge that only one angel can tiptoe down on, or if it is a nice, broad and strong bridge for all the legions of angels to walk down and up, causing that plan to come to pass.

I hope I am giving you a good picture to cling to, to solidify the power of prayer. That is why some people's prayers seem to come to pass quicker than others. Their faith is stronger.

They have greater authority in the spirit, either because of their faith, or because of the authority that God Himself has given to them. That is why I said before that it is the fivefold ministry that should be on the front lines of warfare.

It is because they have the greater authority. They have gone through the stripping, the death, the letting go of self, and God has given them, and trusted them with an authority that can cause those decrees to become established quicker.

Once that bridge has been formed through the power of decree, dare I say, your work has begun.

The process begun at decree, but your work truly takes shape at step three.

Step 3: Persistence – Downloading Your Answers

How many times have we stopped at the promise? How many times have we stopped after one prayer of warfare and telling the devil to go away?

Hooray! You managed to cause the devil to lose his footing for one move in that wrestling match. Did you think that he was going to stay down?

Acts 12:5

Peter was therefore kept in prison, but constant prayer was offered to God for him by the church.

Romans 12:12

Rejoicing in hope, patient in tribulation, continuing steadfastly in prayer;

Downloading the Answer

Your persistent prayers ensure that the download of your blessing continues until completion. We have our angels running up and down. The decree has established it in the earth. The Lord said, "Yes!"

What are you going to do now? You need to get that blessing from heaven to earth. By the way, it is coming through the kingdom of darkness, satan's realm. He would like to think that this world belongs to him.

He has many of his messengers sending arrows your way, making sure that the promise of yours does not come to pass. So, do you really think that a once off prayer time is going to make it happen?

You need persistent prayer. Once you have the promise and the decree, you need to continually, without ceasing, pray, declare, release, insist… until that promise is fully downloaded.

Even in the natural, if you stop a download halfway through, you lose the program and have to start all over. You say to yourself, "Lord, why have you given me the same promise for the last twenty years and I get so far and no further?"

It is because you stopped praying. You did not pray without ceasing. You did not persevere.

It's like this. The angels hear the decree, they go to the start of the bridge, you begin to pray, and they start to run.

They put a brick in place and then they go back to heaven and get another piece of cement. Then they come down and put that one in place and go back to heaven again. With every prayer that you pray, they keep running.

However, halfway through their journey, comes the prince of Persia, the prince of America, or some other prince to hinder them.

Do you know what? Your prayers give them the authority to overcome. However, you stopped praying.

What do the angels respond to again?

They respond to the Word of God. Has the Word of God gone out for you today? I am sure it has gone out in the heavens, but we need it to be manifest in the earth. It is already manifest in heaven.

God already sent the word. God already said, "Yes." The heavens echoed, "I said yes!"

The reality needs to come down to earth.

God's word needs to be spoken in this earth to cause that spiritual promise to manifest. For as long as you declare, release, and continually say that "it will be so" in faith and in accordance to God's will, it is a dog whistle for the angels.

They say, "I hear that. Here is a big uppercut at that prince that is standing in my way. Get out of my way!"

Here is another piece, and another piece, and another piece... until the promise is fully manifest in your life.

> You stop praying, the angels stop working. You stop praying, Satan gets better footing in this wrestling match.

The more faith that you have, the more authority you have and the quicker you will see answers to your prayers.

The first time that you start praying without ceasing, you might be praying for a small thing and it might seem like it's taking forever for those angels to get moving. It is because they have a tiny bridge to work with.

However, you get more authority, faith, hope, and love and then that bridge gets a little broader. This means that every time you pray, more angels are working on your behalf. You are standing against the enemy in a greater measure than before.

You are not little David next to Goliath. You are now Goliath and the enemy looks like David. When you wrestle him, you just need to sit on him, and he is done. At the beginning it does not feel that way though.

That is why you have to persist. You have to keep those angels working. They are the ones doing God's bidding. Are you still releasing God's word, or did you stop after hearing, "Yes, the land is yours..."?

You pray once or twice and say, "Why is this thing not manifesting?"

Did you pray without ceasing? Did you persevere in prayer every minute of the day? Are you continuing to send those prayers up and then releasing those prayers from heaven?

I am not talking about only continuing to go before the Lord, asking Him if you can have this thing when He has already said yes.

When God has already said yes, then you are meant to be talking to your circumstances, saying, "In the name of Jesus, circumstances come into line. Finances, come in line. Body, come in line. This is the promise of God to me and I declare it right now in Jesus' name."

Everywhere I place my feet, God has given to me. Is that not what God said to Joshua? So, Joshua says, "Everywhere I place my feet, this land is mine. This land is mine. This land is mine."

Every time you speak it, the angels work and cause that thing to come to pass. However, we are making the mistake of saying, "Please Lord."

"Yes."

"Please Lord."

"Yes."

You do not need 20 bridges. You just need one. You just need one "Yes" from the Lord. You asked, He said yes and now you need to stand on that promise. That is persistent prayer. That is the power.

When you declare those things that are not as though they were, not once or twice, but persistently without ceasing – you will see results.

Think of the one thing that you want more than anything else in the world. What would you be prepared to do in the natural to get that? What price would you pay? How much money would you give?

How much are you prepared to change? How far would you be prepared to run? How much persistent prayer have you put into that? Did you give up somewhere along the line?

CHAPTER 05 ENTER - INTERCESSION

There is a very big difference between praying for yourself and an intercessor praying. The difference being that the intercessor prays on behalf of others and not on behalf of themselves. That is probably the most outstanding difference between prayer and intercession.

Intercession is never done on your behalf. Jesus is standing on the right hand of the Father interceding for us, right? He does not intercede for Himself. He intercedes for us - for our sins.

That is why prophets are so effective in intercession. Not only are they called of God to help God's people find their place, but they have the authority to call those things into being.

That is why God will call a prophet to come and pray and cause things to be manifest for God's people.

A prophet is not going to come with their ideas, desires and what they want. An intercessor always comes on behalf of others. There are a few ways that an intercessor will approach the Lord.

They may say, "Lord, there is a problem. I see that my brother or sister has a need." They will make that spiritual connection and then God will say, "Yes, I want you to pray," or He will say, "Shut up, I do not want you to pray."

That is the role of the intercessor. If God said no, it is for the person that was doing the original praying to continue to pray, according to God's will, until He says yes. It is not for an intercessor to twist God's arm.

If God says no, it is no. He prays on behalf of someone else, he pleads that case before the Father, the Father says yes or no.

How the Prophet Makes an Impact Through Prayer

Many times, the Lord will say yes, or He will call the intercessor into a specific time of prayer and say, "I have a prayer list for you."

"There are those in my Church who need to be praying this through, but they are not. I need you to make the request on their behalf. My child needs restoration in their marriage, but they are praying the wrong prayer.

They are crying out to me in faith, but they are asking the wrong thing. I need you to pray on their behalf, so that I can give my answer, and you can decree it into the earth. That way the bridge can be established on their behalf."

That is pretty exciting stuff. You can use that spiritual authority to get answers for others. In essence, you are causing conceptions to take place.

Doesn't it sound silly to come to the Lord and ask, "What do you want me to ask you for?"

If the Lord already knows, why does He need us to ask? It is because we need to send up the incense. This is the process and the law that He has set in place.

If He Already Knows, Then Why Ask?

The Scriptures say that He knows our request before we ask, so why does He need us to ask?

> GOD NEEDS US TO ASK SO THAT HE CAN SAY YES AND SO ESTABLISH A BRIDGE, AND THEN RELEASE HIS ANGELS TO DO THE WORK ON OUR BEHALF.

Sometimes somebody cannot pray for themselves because they are in a coma or have been in a car accident. They cannot open their mouth to pray. They may be in a situation where they do not know what to pray. They are stuck.

The Lord will then call on an intercessor to find the words to pray for them. They will then send those prayers up to heaven on that person's behalf. God will give that prophet, that intercessor, the word and they will decree and cause that bridge to be established.

Many times, God will say, "That is good enough. The person involved is praying for themselves now. They are persisting in prayer. You have done what you needed to do."

Other times, God will have that intercessor pray it all the way through to the very end, until they see that thing manifest in the person's life. So, they will conceive that answer in the spirit. They will do warfare.

Speaking from my experience, I have seen many times how someone is praying to the Lord about something. They get the decree and are doing everything they can, but they are engaged in spiritual warfare and are not equipped to handle it. He then calls on me to do the spiritual warfare on their behalf.

The Lord will raise up an intercessor simply for the purpose of doing spiritual warfare on behalf of someone, to remove the hindrances to the prayers that they are already praying.

That is exciting stuff. The Lord uses the prophet specifically because of the level of authority that has been given to them in this earth. That is why God uses prophets so much specifically in the ministry of intercession.

In many situations, the Lord will use a prophet to pray the same thing through again and again. If you are an intercessor and God has you praying for someone and you think that you are finished, but then when you come back to pray again, you see that person again, He is wanting you to download the full answer.

Keep Praying Until the Balance Swings

You need to keep praying until you see the answer or until God tells you to stop. My spiritual mother, who was an incredible intercessor, said it beautifully. She said, "I keep praying until I feel the balance swing."

In the spirit, she would see the need on one side of a balance and her prayer on the other side. God would have her pray for a specific need or person and she would pray, morning, noon, and night. She would pray for hours.

As she prayed, she would see the balance start to tilt in her favor. She said, "I will continue to pray until God tells me to stop, or until one day when I am praying, I feel the balance swing and I know that the prayer has been answered."

Then, she would decree and release it and that thing would come to pass in the earth.

How many of us are spending that much time in persistent prayer, whether in intercession or in prayer for our own problems? We do not see it through to the end.

It is so sad because here is your problem on one end of the scale and here is your prayer on the other side. You probably quit just before the balance swung in your favor.

The download shows 98 percent. You just have two percent to go. Then, you stop praying and the computer powers down. There goes all your hard work. You are back to square one now and you have to start the download all over again.

The angels are arranging specific circumstances.

> FOR YOUR BLESSINGS TO BE MANIFEST, SPECIFIC CIRCUMSTANCES NEED TO BE ARRANGED.

When you stop praying, they get hindered and the circumstances do not get completed and so they have to arrange a new set of circumstances.

That is why it takes so long. I pray that I have challenged you. I do not want you to just pray and unburden yourself before the Lord, which is a beautiful starting point, but to persist in prayer.

Knowing God's Will

You can pray as much as you like, but if you are not praying according to God's will, the angels are not going to respond. You need to know that what you are praying is God's will. There are only two ways to know that.

Number one: Is it in the Word? He said that He will supply our daily needs, our daily bread. That is in His word and I can absolutely stand on His promise and declare it into this earth. I can stand on the Word and say, "Thus says the Word of God. My needs are provided for according to His glory by Christ Jesus."

I can believe it, stand on that, decree it into the earth, cause that bridge to be formed, and continue to stand on it.

Combining Word and Spirit

However, the greater way is when you have a combination of both the Word and the Spirit. This is where you take the relevant scripture, go into the Throne Room of God and say, "Lord, here are my needs, requests, and what I am asking," and then you take time to hear Him say, "Yes, I grant you that. This land belongs to you."

The minute you hear that rhema word, you are not just praying your own thing.

> I ASK YOU TODAY, WHATEVER YOU HAVE BEEN PRAYING FOR, HAVE YOU HEARD GOD SAID YES?

Children just pick these things up so quickly and my son "took me to school" with his faith one day. We were walking through a store called Costco and he saw a bike that he really wanted. He said, "Mommy, please can I have that bike?"

I felt so bad. We were on a tight budget. We really only had money for groceries. I said, "My baby, you are going to have to ask Lord Jesus for this because mommy and daddy do not have the money for it."

He closed his eyes and said, "Please, please Jesus, please."

Then, he opened up his eyes and he said to me, "Mommy, the Lord says yes." He continued to talk about that bike and how the Lord was going to give it to him as we made our way through the aisles.

We thought it was really cute and we carried on with our shopping. We were just about to checkout and my husband received a message on his phone. Someone had put the exact amount of money for that bike into our account.

We could then go and get that bike for him.

It really touched my heart. The Lord had truly said yes. When the Lord says yes, you can believe it. It did not even occur to him after hearing God that he was not going to get his bike.

"We can go back and get my bike now, right?"

"Do not forget my bike before we go, Mom."

"We are going to go back and get the bike now, right?"

"The Lord said yes, I can get my bike."

Do you know what? He was right. The Lord said yes. He heard the Lord for himself. Have you heard the Lord for yourself? Do you have that conviction or are you just praying, hoping, and sending prayers up, but are not hearing what God has to say?

> Hear God speak to you. Get the confirmation that the Lord said yes. If He said yes, then you can decree it into the earth.

"In the name of Jesus, I decree and release. I call that thing to pass right now."

Then do not leave out step three, which is persistent prayer. Daily, hourly, walk up and down. In the early days when this ministry was first born (1999), we would walk up and down the beach with our scripture cards standing on the Word, building our spirit, doing spiritual warfare.

We walked and walked. We walked our way all over the world in the spirit. After being stuck in impossible situations, thinking that there was no way that God could possibly save us from where we were, He pulled us up - these nobodies.

God moved and He can move for you too. He will send His angels to work on your behalf, if you follow through with persistence. However, pray according to His will, know that you have seen it in the spirit and that you have heard Him give it to you in the spirit.

Your fervent prayer avails much, child of God. Persist and you will receive answers!

THE FIVE RULE CHECKLIST

1. Enter the realm of God
2. Receive the promise from God
3. Decree the promise into the earth
4. Engage in spiritual warfare daily (daily stand to)
5. Pray the promise through

We should be au fait with warfare. However, you cannot become comfortable with warfare if you are not prepared to pick up your sword and learn how to use it.

Face the reality. Everyone wants to prophesy and flow in the gifts of the spirit. That is but one kind of warfare... one tiny aspect of warfare. That is like saying, "I am going to enter into a war with only one kind of weapon. I am going to take a sword into a war against cannons."

That is great. I am sure that in close hand-to-hand combat your sword will work, but if someone is taking your troops out with a cannon, I think you need to re-evaluate. That is what we need to do as prophets. It is time that we discover the weapons of our warfare, and what it is going to take to start bringing a change.

Yet, before I run away too much, let me say this one thing. There is a way to get results, in the Church and in your life, without doing warfare. I need you to know something very clearly and I need you to understand why warfare is necessary and what it will and won't do for you.

Although warfare is a powerful weapon, it does not negate the power of faith.

Faith Always Works

Matthew 17:20-21

So Jesus said to them, "...for assuredly, I say to you, if you have faith as a mustard seed, you will say to this mountain, 'Move from here to there,' and it will move; and nothing will be impossible for you.

> *21 However, this kind does not go out except by prayer and fasting."*

If you have this level of faith, you don't need to do warfare. Faith always works. Faith is a powerful, creative force in this earth that always, always works. You could never do a day of warfare but you will eventually see change in your life.

Prayer, persistent prayer, works! That is why I wanted you squared away in prayer first! Learn to pray and you will see results. Now, if you have been on your face before God, time and time again, you have seen God move on your behalf. However, what you might not realize is that when you do warfare, your faith works faster.

Weapons, guns, bows and arrows, they work, and they will hit their target. However, what if you have to shoot through a barrier? What if you have to shoot through an entire army coming your way?

If you keep shooting, you will eventually get through that brick wall. If you keep using your faith again and again and again, things will happen for you. Well… how long do you want to wait?

When we do spiritual warfare, we speed up the process. That is why it is so powerful.

> WARFARE DOES NOT DISPLACE PRAYER OR NEGATE THE POWER OF FAITH. WARFARE GIVES IT WINGS.

It removes the hindrances. When you can put these two aspects together in your life, you will see quicker results in your personal life and in the body of Christ. You will also identify what your mandate is and what God is calling you to do.

You have prayed and prayed and prayed, and you are still waiting. Yes, keep praying or start doing warfare and then you can get your answer quicker. That is what I want to look at in these next chapters with you.

Like we already discussed, prayer is a conversation with the Lord. Prayers go up and you get to the heavenly realm. For those of you who are in our Prophetic School, you know how we teach you to pray and you know the power of prayer, intercession, and decree.

You pray, you make a connection with the Throne Room, and from there, God starts giving you decrees, and you start speaking forth those words into the earth. Those words do not return void, but they take a little bit of time sometimes to "not to return void".

Prayer Vs. Warfare

That is the difference between prayer and warfare. Warfare means using your spiritual authority to remove the work of the enemy. It removes the hindrances to your faith, the blockages to God's promises.

Warfare cannot make the promises come to pass. That is the power of faith. The creative word of God in the earth does that.

Warfare takes away satan's power and the walls that he puts up in your life, that hinder God's promise.

> **PRAYER:** A CONVERSATION WITH THE LORD. PRAYERS GOING UP, GOD'S WORD COMING DOWN
>
> **WARFARE:** USING YOUR SPIRITUAL AUTHORITY TO REMOVE THE WORK OF THE ENEMY

I want you to see the gaps. I want you to see the promises that were not fulfilled. I want you to see the times that God gave you a promise, you prayed, and it never came to pass. I want you to see that there is a better way - a shortcut.

This is a huge part of your place as a believer. Don't underestimate the power of the authority that God has given you as a blood-bought child of God. We have the authority, in the name of Jesus, to overcome every work of darkness. However, it requires actually overcoming.

Just because you are born again, that does not mean that your circumstance is in line with your salvation. Just because God has promised you a piece of land, it does not mean that you possess it.

God promised the children of Israel the Promised Land and they could have sat in Egypt, in slavery for years, bragging about their Promised Land and never eat a fig from it. They had to get themselves out of Egypt and they had to fight for every last fig tree and vine they got.

They also got to live in houses that they did not build. Yet, they had to go and take those houses first. We have become a little complacent in the body of Christ. We have people running around doing warfare, "Let's go and tear down some territorial spirits here and bind that power over there."

First Things First – Is That Your Promised Land?

However, what was the instruction given? Is that your promised land? Can we stand in faith first? Can we go to the Throne Room of God, get the decree, the promise, the blessing, so that we know where our land is at, and then fight for that land?

We should not just fight for any old land that we feel like fighting for. There was a lot of land available back in the day, but God was very specific about the lines and the borders of the Promised Land.

There were many enemies in that time, but God did not give them all of their enemies' land. He was very specific about their portion of land. That was what they were allowed to fight for. Do you even know what your land is before you start running out there and binding demons every five minutes?

You want to go out there and bind the devil, tear down this, and tear down that, but is that your land or are you on someone else's land?

Each one of us have been given our own portion of Promised Land. Even when it comes to calling and mandate, each one of us have been given a very specific piece of land to guard over.

Say that God has given me San Diego or America, then that is my portion of land to fight for. Am I then going to go and walk over to Italy and start binding all the demons of the air there?

Why?! I am just upsetting some other prophet out there who is fighting for that land. I am messing with his strategy.

Have you even been in the Throne Room long enough to know what God has told you in regards to your life, ministry, and mandate, or are you just picking up your sword and saying, "This is handy. Let me just fight?"

Balancing Prayer and Warfare

We need to use faith, the decree that God gives us, our authority, as well as the sword that He has given us to fight the enemy with. We need to bring a little bit of balance in the body of Christ.

It is not all about let's just pray, pray, pray and see what happens. On the other hand, it is not about just fighting every demon in sight and never getting anywhere because let me tell you, you will never run out of demons.

If you are just fighting every demon willy-nilly, there will be a line outside your door, and you will be exhausted. So, let's find some balance here and put spiritual warfare into perspective. In the hand of a skilled warrior, a weapon of war can be devastating. In the hands of an amateur, it is useless.

Let's add some warfare to your persistent prayer and see results… real results… quicker!

CHAPTER 07 INTERNAL WARFARE

> *2 Corinthians 10:3-6*
>
> *For though we walk in the flesh, we do not war according to the flesh.*
> *4 For the weapons of our warfare are not carnal but mighty in God for pulling down strongholds,*
> *5 casting down arguments and every high thing that exalts itself against the knowledge of God, bringing every thought into captivity to the obedience of Christ,*
> *6 and being ready to punish all disobedience when your obedience is fulfilled.*

What you do not realize is that warfare does a lot more than just take down princes of the air. That part is verse four. However, I want you to focus on verse five.

> *5 casting down arguments and every high thing that exalts itself against the knowledge of God, bringing every thought into captivity to the obedience of Christ,*

Before you can go attacking demons out there, you need to start with internal warfare. God has given you a promise and it is not coming to pass. Maybe you even wake up in the morning and it feels so heavy. This applies especially for those of you in full-time ministry.

It seems like someone sent out a memo somewhere and every demon in hell decided that they are going to come at you today. It feels like there is such a cloud of heaviness around your head. Your mind is foggy. You are distracted. You are irritable.

It is like the Lord's voice suddenly becomes fuzzy. It is not clear. You know that He wants to talk to you, but you are thinking, "Am I missing something? Am I out of line with what God wants to do?"

You start looking at yourself and thinking, "Maybe I sinned? Maybe I should not have sworn at that driver? Maybe I should have been nicer to that sister at church and not lost my temper? Maybe I should not have got frustrated with my leader when he corrected me."

You get all introspective. However, I want to direct you to something interesting.

Wrestling for the Message

We touched on this before, but let's take it deeper. I am going to share a passage from Daniel with you. You can read up more on it on your own because I do not want to put too much scripture here. In this part of the passage, Daniel had been fasting for an answer from the Lord.

He had already been getting messages from the Lord, but suddenly nothing was coming. So, he is fasting and praying, fasting and praying, "Where is this message?"

I want you to see what happens.

> ### Daniel 10:12-14
>
> *Then he said to me, "Do not fear, Daniel, for from the first day that you set your heart to understand, and to*

humble yourself before your God, your words were heard; and I have come because of your words.
13 But the prince of the kingdom of Persia withstood me twenty-one days; and behold, Michael, one of the chief princes, came to help me, for I had been left alone there with the kings of Persia.
14 Now I have come to make you understand what will happen to your people in the latter days, for the vision refers to many days yet to come."

What was the problem? Was it that God was not talking? Had God not sent the answer, or had His word not gone forth?

No! God's word had gone forth. That word was being hindered and held back.

Was Daniel out of line or not righteous enough that God did not answer right away? Not at all. Rather, he was engaged in some spiritual warfare.

Sign of Warfare: God's Voice Is Not Clear

When you start experiencing this kind of blockage in your spirit, it is not God's voice that is the problem. It is that there is so much noise, interference, and restriction put on you by the enemy that you cannot hear God's voice.

Why do we always put the blame on God?

"Well... God is not talking to me at the moment. God has put me on the shelf. God is just holding me at arm's length."

God never stops talking!

I wake up in the morning and my ten-year-old son comes running up to me and says, "Mommy, can I have breakfast?"

Do I just turn my back on him, walk away, and pretend he is not there? Would I continue to act that way towards him for days?

What kind of mother would I be if I did that? Do you think that your Heavenly Father is any different?

Let me tell you very plainly. If God's voice suddenly stops, it is not God who stopped talking. You are experiencing some warfare. Yet, you get so caught up in your own righteousness and sanctification that you do not recognize that God is talking but you are just not hearing Him.

You need to ask why you are not hearing Him. It is very likely that you got out of the way, or hung up the phone, and you are not getting the message. However, even if that is the case, it is still warfare. Who do you think inspired you to get off track?

God has not stopped speaking to you. If the word is no longer coming, you have something hindering that word. I just love that illustration in Daniel because he was perfectly in line with the will of God, but yet he still had to wait.

What was crazy was that he could not do spiritual warfare like we do. It says that he just kept praying and fasting. He did it with pure faith. Do you see that? He continued with pure faith, believing in God, praying and asking for the answer.

The New Testament Difference

He prayed, prayed, and prayed, and eventually his faith won out. The archangel came, did warfare for him in the heavenlies, and the answer eventually came through. We have something in the New Testament that Daniel never did.

We have authority in the name of Jesus. He did not have the authority back then to give angels or demons commands. He did not have authority over death and hell because Jesus had not yet come to give that authority to man.

No man had authority over death and hell until Jesus rose from the dead. So, he could not say, "That's it. In the name of Jesus, I bind you, Prince of Persia" so that the word could be released.

That is why I call this internal warfare. When you start doing this kind of spiritual warfare, you eventually get to the place where you hear God above the noise. The noise no longer restricts you from hearing His voice.

Get the Word First

You cannot just go fighting demons out there when you are not in line with God's will. You can't fight until you have orders from the General. Just because I have a sword does not mean that I go out there and use it at random.

I am in submission to the General of my army in the kingdom of God. Until He has given me those orders, what right do I have to use any of my gifts, the tools I have, or any army, against anything or anyone?

> WE ARE AN ARMY AND EACH OF US NEEDS TO GET OUR OWN COMMAND FROM GOD.

When we can do that, we will walk in unity. Yet, if you keep just using your sword for the sake of using your sword and are going into territories you shouldn't, you are going to get a major backlash. You are going to get taken out by the enemy.

Why? Is it because God is making you suffer?

No. It is because you did not listen. God never sent you onto that battlefield in the first place. So, when you start doing spiritual warfare, the first thing that starts happening is that the message makes its way through.

That is why spiritual warfare begins with us. It begins with bringing our own minds into line, binding our own thoughts.

The more you rise up in ministry, the more people you have under you, the bigger the attacks. All the weights, thoughts, fears, guilt… start coming at you. There are some days you wake up and think, "Lord, I cannot hear you through everyone's needs, my mistakes, what I need to do, what I have not done, the list of jobs that I have to…"

The Lord said to me, "Tell those thoughts to shut up."

"Yeah, but Lord, I need to take care."

"Just bind those thoughts. They are not in line with my will. What you are thinking and feeling, that feeling of self-pity, the guilt and fear, I am sorry, Colette, but it is not in line with my will. So, can you just bind it, tell it to shut up, and let's get on with it?"

So... I started doing that.

"I bind you, spirit of fear. I bind you, guilt, panic, and stress. In the name of Jesus, Colette, you come in line with the mind of Christ. Thoughts, you be quiet now in Jesus' name. Be still. I bring every thought into captivity. I cast down every one of these imaginations that are attacking my mind that I cannot understand. I bring you in line in Jesus' name."

The minute you do that, what is already in your spirit will come out. You do not need to fight for the word of God. That is not what this warfare is about. It is not fighting for the word of God.

> INTERNAL WARFARE IS ABOUT REMOVING THE HINDRANCES TO THE WORD THAT GOD HAS ALREADY GIVEN TO YOU.

When you can do that, you will realize that the battle is not yours. You just need to come in line. You just need to come in line with what God wants. You have a whole army standing behind you.

Getting in Line With the Message - The Garden of Gethsemane

I am reminded of Jesus in the Garden of Gethsemane. If you want to know what this internal warfare looks like, I want to point you there. Jesus knew what He had to do. He knew what would come of what He had to do, but He also knew the price that He would have to pay to do it.

He travailed in the garden. He struggled with His flesh, and His will. At the end, after sweating blood, He said, "Father, not my will, but yours be done."

Then, He was ready for warfare. This is when He was ready to go down into hell and get the keys of death and hell and bring them back for us. Yet, it started with the Garden of Gethsemane.

None of us want to go through the Garden of Gethsemane. We just want to march into satan's kingdom, rattle the gates of hell, and set all the captives free.

Have you gone through the garden yet? Have you brought yourself in line with God's will?

There is a struggle. You know, we always think that the greatest struggles we face are with our desires, but we are wrong. The greatest struggles we face are with our insecurities, guilts, fears, shortcomings, and everything that makes us feel useless and less than who we are.

That is our struggle. That is our garden. It is what we can't do, not what we can do. The things where we feel inadequate. God says to Moses, "You go out there and speak to Pharaoh."

Moses felt inadequate standing at the burning bush. He had a back and forth with God before he was ready to face the enemy. That is the kind of place God needs to bring you to because you are not ready to hear His word yet. You are too busy struggling with yourself.

"I don't know if I can do this. I don't think I am strong enough for this. I am not anointed enough for this. What if they come against me? I do not know if I am ready to handle that."

These are the struggles we face more than anything else. That is why this kind of warfare is essential. You need to discover that it is not by might, nor by your power, but it is by His spirit that you will overcome.

That is only going to happen if you go through the garden and you begin to fight for your promises, according to God's will.

Fight for the Promises!

Listen, just because God gave you a promise, it doesn't mean it is coming to pass.

"God gave me a promise. He gave me the promised land."

I am happy for you, but are you willing to fight for it?

"God told me that I would go to this church and that He would pour out His spirit on the church. He said that he would bring revival to His church."

"God promised me finances, healing, a child."

Yet, you are sitting there and waiting for the promise to come out of heaven.

Note for the Prophets: Listen, especially if you are a prophet, "die already" to that. It is never going to happen by giving one word and waiting. Sorry guys, if anyone is positioned at the front lines, it is you, prophet.

It is not just going to come to you. Promises will not just drop out of the sky. Rather you will be called to fight for every single promise that God has given you.

Abraham had to give up his son. David had to slay Goliath, and then run to the Cave of Adullam. Do you know how many men David had to kill to get that throne?

God promised Apostle Paul that he would reach the Gentiles. Did it just get handed to him? No, he had to fight. He had to run for his life. He had to get up time and again. He had to get out of prison only to get thrown back into prison. He had to fight his way through the justice system. He had to do everything in his power again and again, to see the promise through.

Can we smash this wishy-washy thinking of, "If it's God's will, it's God's bill?"

If I hear anyone say that to me, I swear, we are going to have a talk. No, it is *your* bill. We are servants and He is our master.

His will is our command, not His bill.

If He says to go and take the land, then you go and take the land, but start with getting yourself in line. Submit yourselves therefore to God, resist the devil and he will flee from you (James 4:7).

It starts with getting yourself sorted before you can go "out there."

Fruit of Internal Warfare

I love the fruit of the internal warfare when you get this right. You will hear the voice of the Lord again. That is probably the best part. When you start doing this kind of warfare and wrestle a while to get yourself in line, you will start hearing the voice of the Lord again. You will begin receiving revelation concerning the blockages in your life.

In fact, you will stumble onto them. People will knock on your door out of the blue or someone will act out of character and reveal something that was hidden. You will say, "You mean to tell me that this is what you were thinking this whole time?"

You end up finding an underlying current in your ministry that was poisoning you that you had no clue about. Suddenly, things become uncovered and your faith begins to ride high.

I love the scripture that refers to our faith as a mustard seed. You do not need a lot of faith, but when you have a heavy weight on your faith, it is hard to see the fruit of it.

> WHEN YOU START REMOVING THE WEIGHTS ON YOUR FAITH, THE FAITH THAT YOU ALREADY HAVE WILL SKYROCKET.

It is good to develop your faith. However, if you want the shortcut, which is what I am giving you now, then you need to do some warfare. Then, the faith that you already have will grow naturally.

You will leave those times of prayer feeling, "We can do this, guys!" Before, you woke up feeling overwhelmed and exhausted spiritually and emotionally.

You were tired, hurt, frustrated, and your mustard seed of faith was nowhere to be found. Yet, when you start doing this warfare, suddenly, you will start receiving a possibility thinking.

"We can do this! I am going to get up again, try again, and overcome again."

You have been trying, in your willpower, to push your faith out and it is hard. On the other hand, you could just do the warfare and your faith would rise up out of you naturally.

Spirit of Heaviness Will Lift

Then, you will notice that the clouds of heaviness will lift. That is my favorite part. You know that spirit of heaviness that you often feel in your home, ministry or church?

You feel like you stand up to worship and you have to push through the praise. You stand up to preach and you have to push the message out. You think, "Is anybody even listening to any of this?" It feels like you are hitting wall after wall.

When you do this kind of warfare, that heaviness lifts and then you can pick up your sword and direct it exactly to where the enemy is hiding. You are no longer affected by the warfare. It does not mean that the warfare is all gone, it just means you are no longer affected by it.

You need to understand that just because you feel heaviness, see demons and feel oppression, that it means you should react and attack wildly. For those of you who flow in the gift of discerning of spirits, you are very much aware of what is going on in the spirit. Because you are so sensitive to what is going on, it can feel overwhelming. You might make the mistake of thinking the enemy has the upper hand because the oppression is so strong.

Do not allow what you feel in the spirit to be the driving force of the warfare you do. Fight according to God's instructions.

> DO NOT PICK UP YOUR SWORD JUST BECAUSE OF WHAT YOU SENSE. PICK UP YOUR SWORD BECAUSE OF THE MARCHING ORDERS YOU WERE HANDED!

You Will Feel Spiritual Clarity

So get yourself out of the warfare first. Get to where your spirit is at peace, where you are not feeling demons, seeing them in your sleep, and waking up to them every day.

This is especially valid for those of you who are evangelistic and functioning in that type of ministry a lot. It can get overwhelming when all you see is what the enemy is doing.

Let's get you separated from that so that you can see clearly in the spirit and not just feel demons and heaviness all the time. This kind of internal warfare is your ticket to bringing clarity.

The Anointing Never Left

From there it is easy to get into the Lord's presence. If you have been battling to feel the anointing tangibly, then you just need to do a little warfare. God's presence is still there, and you still have the indwelling of the Holy Spirit. He has not gone anywhere.

Bringing Your Soul Into Line

Can we stop blaming God for the devil's work? Our feelings are so easily manipulated. What warfare does, is it gets our soul (our mind, emotions, and will) in line with the will of God.

When we do that, our spirit can come to peace and we can see the real enemy. Then, your work really begins. Now, you are ready. You are ready to put on your armor. You are ready to attack the enemy "out there". It is time for prophetic warfare.

FRUIT OF INTERNAL WARFARE SUMMARY

1. You will hear the Lord's voice again.
2. You will get the revelation of your blockage/open door.
3. Your faith will begin to ride high.
4. The cloud of heaviness will lift.
5. You will find it easy to get into the Lord's presence.

CHAPTER 08 Prophetic Warfare

> *Ephesians 6:11-12*
>
> *Put on the whole armor of God, that you may be able to stand against the wiles of the devil.*
> *12 For we do not wrestle against flesh and blood, but against principalities, against powers, against the rulers of the darkness of this age, against spiritual hosts of wickedness in the heavenly places.*

Now, we're talking! Now, I am ready to take the devil down out there because I am not in the middle of that warfare anymore. I am riding as a victor out onto that battlefield with my flag held high. I am not going out as a little pawn, half-defeated, slogging my way through the battlefield and being taken out every five minutes.

Instead I am leading from a position of authority and knowing what God wants. I am not heading into the battlefield half dead. I am not going to be productive that way. Get yourself in line first.

> TRUE WARFARE BEGINS ONCE YOUR SPIRIT IS IN LINE WITH GOD'S WILL.

Now, the warfare can really begin, and you can start seeing some things happening.

Warfare for Your Circumstances

This is where you start warring for your circumstances. This is where you stand and do warfare on behalf of your ministry. I will give you very clear steps when I get to making it practical in the next chapter, of exactly how you need to do that.

This is when you redirect your prayer to start speaking to those circumstances and calling them in line. This is when you say, "Mountain, be removed. You, circumstances, come in line with the will of Jesus. I remove the spirit of infirmity in my family. I stand against the spirit of poverty in my family."

You know, because your spirit is in line, your faith is going to ride high. Just think about the power of your double-edged sword!

You do the internal warfare, your faith rises up, and you feel the presence of God. From there you receive direction from God. You take all that faith, add a sword to it, and send the word out.

Isn't this powerful? I have seen this work. It is powerful and you will tangibly feel that word going from you. You will tangibly see things happening in your circumstances.

You pray to the Lord about your finances. You pray to the Lord about your family and your health. You pray and He gives you a promise. Now, have you done the internal warfare so that you can say, "Body, come in line in the name of Jesus?"

"You, thoughts of fear, I bind you and refuse to entertain you. You will come in line with the promise and will of God, now!"

Do you feel that faith rising up? If so, then you are now ready. Your faith is riding high and you feel the presence of the Lord, and you are at peace in your spirit. Now, you are ready to do real warfare.

Come on Prophets... Are You Ready for This?

I am not just talking about your personal life here. If you are a prophet, then you need to take it a step further. You need to be doing this on behalf of others. Yet, how can you fight on their behalf if you do not even have your own spirit in line?

When God puts a prophet in a ministry, a group, under a pastor or apostle, they usually want to jump in and do warfare.

You and I both know how much we love the prophetic warfare messages, prophet. You know what I am talking about. We love giving the devil a good kick in the butt. We get in there and march around the walls of Jericho. We bind him for the sake of binding him, just because it feels good to bind him.

That is great. Get it out. Practice a little. Stand in your authority. However, then you need to do something that is going to work.

> YOU NEED TO TAKE ALL THOSE TOOLS, WEAPONS, AND "SHOUTS OF HALLELUJAH" AND MAKE THEM WORK.

So, can we just be a little more practical about the direction of our prayer and pray according to what God wants?

We work with many prophets that God has sent into churches that do not believe in the gifts of the Spirit, never mind the fivefold ministry. They feel so dead spiritually that they are singing from hymnals. (Not that I don't love those old hymns. I'm just saying that God has a way of reaching each generation afresh!)

I am talking about Catholic churches, Baptist churches, and Methodist churches. God sends a prophet, a fiery, crazy prophet into that church and He knows that they will be like Jeremiah. The prophet will not be accepted.

Their gift is going to be kicked out the back door and they are going to be told to sit down and shut up. They will end up thinking, "What am I doing here, Lord?"

You are there to do warfare, prophet! You are in the back of the church doing warfare. Get over yourself. Get over the fact that your gift is not recognized. Who do you need to recognize it exactly?

I am pretty sure that God sees your gift and the devil does too. So, I think we are okay. Who is the real enemy here, the body of Christ or your pride? Can you sit in the back of a church and do nothing but intercede and do warfare?

Can you sit there and bind the spirit of religion, the spirit of heaviness, and the blindness in that place again and again, until you see the power of God move there?

> WE NEED MORE PROPHETS IN DEAD CHURCHES.

We need more prophets where it is dry and dark. We need you to pick up your sword, super-spy, and for you to get in there where satan does not see you are getting in.

Who would expect a prophet in the back of a Catholic church?

Yet, I have seen it done and I have seen God move in those churches. I have seen people suddenly become spirit-filled out of nowhere, in those churches. It was because of the prophet in the back doing spiritual warfare.

This is the kind of warfare that I am talking about and the kind of authority that God wants to give you. However, can we get ourselves in line first with the thoughts of God, and can we start removing the hindrances to the move of God in the Church?

Get This Memo Prophet

Think of it like this. You are a business owner and there is a multi-faceted job that needs to get done. You have two teams in your business.

The first team is efficient and gets their jobs done on time. They pay attention to detail and are reliable.

The second team never gets their job done, and they are always squabbling amongst one another.

The first team pushes the vision forward and are doing great.

As that business owner, if you want your business to grow as a whole, where are you going to concentrate most of your effort?

Are you going to concentrate on helping the team that is flourishing?

No! You are going to reach out to the team that is bickering and killing the vision, so that you can get them up to speed with everybody else, right? This way, you can move forward together.

Our Heavenly Father wants a well-structured and efficient Body. Throughout history, He has always reached out to heal the broken. Reached out to the one who was lost. So just as that business owner, He will focus efforts where help is needed most.

Be the Light in the Darkness

So many prophets want to be sent to a prophetic church. That's great. Let's add you to a group that has already got the memo. You are useless there. Useless! Prophet, you are useless in a prophetic church… seriously!

Can you please go where it's dead? You are useful there because there are not many of you there. You have a light to shine in the darkness. You are needed where they are behind, bickering, and struggling under a cloud of heaviness.

I am not saying that it is going to be easy. Who said anything about it being easy? What definition of the word "war" don't you understand?

Can we get a little "black and white", and separate the sheep from the goats? What kind of prophet are you? One that really wants to see change in the body of Christ or one that just wants to flow in your prophetic gifts every five minutes?

If you want to do that, then just go and prophesy at home. You are useless to the body of Christ. I am sorry. I know that this is harsh, but this is a memo to prophets here, and we understand the concept of "black or white". That is just the way it is.

You may be useful to yourself or your family that you always prophesy to, but what about your family out there?

> WHEN ARE WE GOING TO BE USEFUL OUT THERE, WHERE IT IS DARK? DO WE HAVE THE COURAGE TO GO OUT THERE WHERE IT IS DARK AND DO WARFARE THERE?

You do not take a land that is flourishing and that you own. You take a land that is dark and that you don't own. I want to challenge you because God has given us so much more than what we see in our lives and churches.

"I want to go prophesy in front of the crowds where everybody will receive my prophetic word."

That is not where they need the prophetic word! They need the prophetic word where it is dead and dull, and where the spirit of God is not being given license to flow. That is where we need to engage in warfare.

When we start doing that kind of warfare, we are going to see circumstances change. Doors will start opening and connections will start being made.

Prophets and Apostles Working Together

Do you know what is cool? (I am speaking now as an apostle.) When you have a team of prophets praying and doing this kind of warfare, you suddenly start getting revelation. It's quite miraculous. When the prophets start to pray, I start having dreams and then when I go to speak with the Lord, He starts laying things out clearly.

Whereas before, things felt like, "What is the next step, Lord? I don't know what we should be doing next." You struggle and struggle and then suddenly... BOOM!! It is like a blueprint just falls from heaven.

When that happens, everyone thinks I am so anointed. However, I know the truth. I know that the revelation did not come because of me and my great revelation and anointing. That revelation came because the prophets were doing warfare. They were praying and I got the pattern.

Once that happens, then together, we can implement it. If you want the pastor to get revelation, do you think your prophetic word is going to do it? Can I just pop that little bubble right here?

the outskirts of Israel and took the enemy down for Saul, so that by the time he took the throne, those enemies had already been subdued. That is the authority God's given you.

War Against Principalities

We are doing warfare on the wrong plane here. We are doing warfare against man. We are doing warfare against people instead of principalities, powers, and those that are blocking those people from getting the revelation from the Lord.

God could get through to Saul in the times it was needed most. Yes, Saul was stubborn, and he still wanted to kill David every five minutes, but at the end of the day, God took care of Saul so David did not have to.

We underestimate the power of faith. When you do this kind of warfare, people will be added and removed, and you will move towards your promise. Things will start to change.

When you do this kind of warfare, suddenly somebody will be appointed, and somebody will be removed. Suddenly, someone will be added to your life and someone will be removed from your life.

It is all to get you in line with the promise that God has for you. It is actually quite exciting.

Proof of Warfare: Circumstances Will Shift

Let's take a really practical example now. Say now that you are doing warfare for your health. You may suddenly find a doctor that has a simple solution for you. There you are, praying and praying for your miraculous healing, and it may even come that way. However, God may move on your circumstances to put you in the pool of Bethesda where you can be healed.

Why don't you leave it up to Him?

When you do this kind of warfare, things will start to happen, circumstances will start to shift. You may lose a job. Well, that's good. If you have been doing warfare, then it seems that you need a new one. That is not where the blessing is at and you need to move.

Circumstances will begin to change. When you are in a church or ministry and you are doing this kind of warfare, those are the kinds of changes that you will see. You will start seeing those shifts.

"Oh, I don't know what is happening in our church. There was a church split!"

"Oh my goodness, I don't know what is happening. This new leader was appointed, and the other leader was taken down. What is God doing?"

God always wanted to do it. You just removed the obstacles through your warfare and gave God license in that place and now He started to bring change in those circumstances. It is actually quite exciting, if you stop for a moment and think about it.

You can save the world right from your community with this. We don't need to go out there. Let's just start right where we are, shall we? There is enough work to do. Wherever God plants you, that is your community.

Wherever God sets you, that is your place to set up those battlements, pick up your weapons, and to start doing warfare against the enemy.

FRUIT OF PROPHETIC WARFARE SUMMARY

1. A change to circumstances
2. Doors open and connections are made
3. Your apostle/pastor will get fresh direction and revelation for the ministry
4. People will be added and removed from the ministry
5. You will move TOWARD the promises

CHAPTER 09 MAKING IT PRACTICAL

You know what warfare can do for you. Let's go through some quick steps here. This is the part of the book where you take notes and then apply what you learn! Re-visit these principles. Teach them to your local church and your family. Stand on the land together and watch God move!

To fully apply everything in this book, I encourage you to work through it again with the matching Workbook to make all the principles stick.

1. Internal Warfare – Your Garden of Gethsemane

2 Corinthians 10:5

casting down arguments and every high thing that exalts itself against the knowledge of God, bringing every thought into captivity to the obedience of Christ,

We start with internal warfare. Let's get ourselves in line. Cast down your imaginations.

"Father, I submit myself to you. I bring every thought into line. I bind that fear and guilt and I put that frustration aside."

You can start with everyone you were offended with. That is the biggest spirit blocker ever. Your judgments and offenses kill you and strangle the anointing of God in your life.

Can you also put bitterness on the cross? If you want to get your sword sharp, then you need to get rid of the enemy's weapons so that you can put on the armor of God. You are carrying the wrong weapon.

"Father forgive me for being offended. I let that judgment go."

"I put on the altar the fact that I am panicking that the rent is due, and I have not paid it. I let go of how I feel."

"I don't know what to do about my marriage. I feel frustrated and lost, but I give you control again Father."

"I call every thought into line! Every imagination to submit to the Lord!"

"I quiet those thoughts of fear and guilt! Come into line, soul!"

This is really an emptying. It is your Garden of Gethsemane, where you strip, let go, and you bring your spirit into line. Do as David always did and say, "Soul, come to peace." He used to sing to himself as well.

Come to peace. Put away your striving. It may take a bit of time. It may help if you do the bulldozing project. (I will share the project at the end of the chapter.)

This helps to get your mind off all the stuff that is going on around you in the natural. It is a powerful way to get your spirit into line, and to enter into rest.

2. Now, Pray the Vision Through

Habakkuk 2:3

*For the vision is yet for an appointed time;
But at the end it will speak, and it will not lie.
Though it tarries, wait for it;
Because it will surely come,
It will not tarry.*

Once you have done that, if you are in a ministry, are you working towards a common goal? What is the vision of your apostle or pastor?

What direction have you and your spouse received from the Lord?

If you are in a church, I am not asking you if you like or agree with their vision. I am not even asking you if you want to be a part of it. I am asking you what it is, and if God has put you there. Did God put you in that church? Did He put you under that leader?

If so, then the next thing that you will start doing is warfare for that vision. You start binding that prince that is holding back the word.

> HERE IS A QUESTION FOR THOSE WHO HAVE BEEN ALONG THE WAY FOR A WHILE: WHEN GOD GIVES YOU A VISION, DOES IT ALWAYS COME TO YOU PERFECTLY FROM THE VERY FIRST DAY OR DOES IT EVOLVE?

It evolves. God reveals more, the more you pray. It comes to you as a lamp to your feet. Now, because of our circumstances and upbringing, we always see so many things in the vision that we want to see.

It takes us a while to get to the point where we are like, "Oh, so that is what God meant."

Give the Apostle a Break…

Give the apostle a break. He has given you what he's got, but if you started doing warfare for that vision, he would get the rest of the picture. You would know then that you were in line with God's will.

Instead of fighting the vision and the man, why don't you fight the demons of hell so that he can start seeing clearly again?

God put you into that ministry or church for a reason. What is his vision? Remove every hindrance to that vision. Do you know how many people are likely speaking against him, prophesying against him, standing against him, and saying negative things behind his back?

If you are a leader, that is just how it goes. I do not care what an amazing leader you are, there are people who do not like you. It is just the nature of the ministry. Are you putting yourself in the gap?

"I stand against every negative word that has been spoken against this man. I remove every hindrance in Jesus' name. Satan, you will loose your hold. I speak blessing on his finances, healing to his body, and clarity to his mind in Jesus name. Satan, lose your hold on his mind. I rebuke you and I remove every hindrance."

You must start praying in the direction of the vision. Maybe the vision is for him to start a soup kitchen and you don't care much for it. However, it is his vision. Just do warfare!

"I speak forth a property so that he can start this ministry. Even now, in the name of Jesus, I call out every one of those members that are needed to work in this vision. I prepare them in Jesus' name. Satan, I remove this hindrance where you are holding them back."

When you start doing warfare and praying, he is going to get clarity and you are going to see the vision from his perspective, like you never have before. You have not seen it correctly because you have never gotten into the realm of the spirit to see it from God's perspective. You were just judging his vision with human understanding and you did not get it.

> WHEN YOU GET TO THE PLACE OF DOING WARFARE, YOU START TO SEE WHAT THAT MAN SEES.

Suddenly, you are useful. It doesn't matter whether your leader sees that you are useful or not, God does. That is really what counts. You will start having an impact.

Take It to The World

What you do not realize, is that as you do this warfare, you position yourself to get revelation! This same principle applies to every area of your life.

> **Romans 13:1**
>
> *Let every soul be subject to the governing authorities. For there is no authority except from God, and the authorities that exist are appointed by God.*

How about your workplace? Are you praying through your boss's vision for the company? Are you praying through your husband's desire for your family? Are you praying through your President's dreams for your nation?

Don't you realize that when you start to pray these visions through, if they are out of line, you give license to the Holy Spirit to change the vision! When you stand in the gap, you give the Lord license to bring real change.

"Lord I speak your blessing on this business and open these doors of opportunity"

"I speak an abundance of jobs and commerce in my country!"

"Lord I thank you for the house that my husband wants for our family."

Get the idea? Pray according to the vision. Position yourself! This is easy if you paid attention in the first step, to get yourself out of the way first.

3. Get Revelation!

Once you are properly positioned, you will begin to see the blockages that are hindering the vision. You will start getting words of wisdom, words of knowledge, and seeing people that should not be there. You will start seeing the underlying works of the enemy.

For those of you who flow in the gift of discerning of spirits, you will see demonic bondages, princes of the air, spirits of strife... whatever the blockage is. For those of you who are along the way in your prophetic call, you know what I am talking about.

You get down to do this kind of warfare and you might suddenly start seeing a spirit of lust or witchcraft! From here you are in a position to cause real damage to the kingdom of darkness.

If you have just recently come to hear the voice of God for yourself, you might "feel" more than you see in the spirit. To grow in how to hear the Lord, grab my book *How to Hear the Voice of God*

> TO BE EFFICIENT IN WARFARE, YOU NEED REVELATION.

You might begin praying the vision through, but do not go on to step four until you have begun to receive revelation.

That revelation may come to you in a vision or a dream. You might get it through the Word or via an inner knowing in your spirit. Either way, do not enter into active warfare without arming yourself.

Follow The Revelation

As you are praying the vision through, it is like getting on a boat in a meandering river. As you float down the river, you will feel the subtle rocking and shift of the boat as it floats.

Keep on the boat! If it floats left, then follow it. Don't fight the current.

> REVELATION IS PROGRESSIVE. IN OTHER WORDS, YOU WILL NOT GET THE FULL PICTURE ALL AT ONCE.

You will begin with just a sense of, "I feel that this vision needs to change."

So then pray it through. "Lord I thank you for changing this vision according to your will." After that, you might feel that something needs to be added.

Simple enough! "Lord I add to this vision what you want added."

Once you pray that though perhaps you see someone in the spirit or you get a word of knowledge that for this vision to be complete, someone needs to get involved. Fantastic! "I open the doors for this person to join and be involved in this vision!"

If you are used to flowing in visions, even better. Simply pray that vision through until it changes. Say you are praying that vision through for your new house.

As you are praying, you see chains around the house. Ok, that's easy. "I bring this blockage to you Lord. I reveal whatever it is that is holding our house back!"

There you go! You keep praying that through until you see the chains broken over that house. After that, you might very well see something else. Be sensitive and follow the gentle rocking of that boat. Allow the river of the Holy Spirit to direct you to His destination.

Do not just "hit it and run." No, pray the revelation through until you no longer get any more.

4. Rebuke the Enemy

"Where is that demon coming from? I expose you, in Jesus' name, and I bind you."

If you are working with a leader that you can share those things with, that is fantastic. However, even if the leader does not receive it, it does not matter. You just do warfare. You know what God has shown you.

That revelation is going to start to show through fruit in circumstances. As you get that revelation, continue to bind the work of the enemy again and again. It is very powerful. Do you see the progression?

> THIS IS WAR. YOU DO NOT JUST GO OUT INTO WAR AND SHOOT STUFF AT RANDOM.

You must have a focus, get yourself in line, know your authority in the name of Jesus. You must face the enemy, see who he is, bind him. Then, you will start seeing things shifting in an incredible way in whatever ministry or circumstance you are in.

You might see something demonic holding on to the chains of your house. "I bind you satan! I remove this blockage in the spirit!"

"I rebuke the spirit of poverty in this country! You must bow!"

"I expose the hidden intentions in this company that are hindering its blessing, in Jesus name!"

"I expose and rebuke the spirit of strife that I see rampant in this church!"

Now is really the time to get real with the enemy. You know what God wants. You know the vision. You have revelation on what is hindering that vision. So, pick up your sword and tell the enemy where he can go!

This is the most powerful part of all and vital to removing any hindrances to the promises God has given.

5. Call Circumstances Into Line

Romans 4:17

> ...God, who gives life to the dead and calls those things which do not exist as though they did;

When you are done binding the work of the enemy, there is something else that you need to do. You need to call circumstances into line. You see, for these promises to come to pass, circumstances need to come in line.

For the money to flow in a certain way, circumstances need to shift so that the money can be paid out. Call the circumstances into line!

"In Jesus' name, I stand against the system that is resisting this move of God. You, circumstances, come into line. I put the right people in the right place, at the right time."

"I put those Mordecai's and Esther's in the courts of the king so that they can speak the right word at the right time to tear up, pull down, build up."

"I call the medical system into line, so that a cure can be found and the healing can flow!"

"I thank you Lord for putting the right people in the right place in the entertainment industry."

"I call the circumstances into line to ensure a quick release of that paperwork and signing of that contract, in Jesus name."

"Circumstances – you come into line now with the will of God!"

Come on, we can do this! Everybody wants to tear down, tear down, tear down, but what about build up, build up, build up? Can we do some building up and establishing?

Let's start seeing some change.

6. Prophesy God's Will Into the Earth!

Just before you think you are all done. The last step is for you to prophesy.

> ### Ezekiel 13:2
>
> *"Son of man, prophesy against the prophets of Israel who prophesy, and say to those who prophesy out of their own heart, 'Hear the word of the Lord!' "*

At first you think, "He must have had a big prophetic conference, invited all the prophets, stood up behind the pulpit and prophesied at them."

How realistic does that sound to you?

In all of Israel, can you see Ezekiel, the prophet who, by the way, was not very popular, having a huge prophetic gathering? Would you want to attend? No one liked the man! I don't think so.

He prophesied in faith. He did not have a conference and prophesy face-to-face to the prophets. He prophesied to them in the spirit. It did not matter whether they heard it or not. He wrote it down and it was good enough.

You have stood in your authority, released those words, bound those demons, and removed blockages. Before all is said and done though, it is time for God to speak. This is the most powerful warfare of all, and it is the step that we all miss.

I am not talking about decree necessarily. I am speaking about prophetic words of warfare. Words that you speak into the earth on God's behalf. You are His mouthpiece that He sends that word out from.

the spirit. Then, you can start seeing a breakthrough in your life.

Do something! Do something about your circumstances. Do something about your church. Do something about your ministry. Stop just sitting around and thinking that things are going to fall out of the sky.

I have given you the steps and the structure, but you hold the tools in your own hand. The next step… is entirely up to you.

Making It Practical Summary

1. Internal Warfare – Get in Line
2. Pray the Vision Through
3. Get Revelation!
4. Rebuke the Enemy
5. Call Circumstances into Line
6. Prophesy!

Bulldozing Project

Project Objective:

There is only one way that faith increases and that is by hearing the rhema word of God. A powerful weapon for mentor and intern alike, this project will increase faith and assist in an answer to prayer.

Make note that this project is not a magic wand. Rather it is a tool used to increase faith. Faith in turn yields the answer to prayer.

Project Profile:

- Ideal for prophets in training
- Should be mandatory for intercessors
- Ideal for believers believing God for something specific
- Spiritual maturity

Bulldozing Project

My son loves bulldozers. If there is one on a construction site, he makes us slow down the car so that he can get a better look. It is some impressive equipment. It can face a pile of rubble or even a heap of sand and push it over with no effort at all.

That is the picture you want to keep in mind as you approach this project. What is your problem today? What are you struggling with? This project will give you the bulldozer you need to run right through these problems.

Never forget, the Lord is moved by faith. Without faith it is impossible to please Him. So, do you want an answer to your prayer? Then you need to get your faith into gear! Until you "know that you know" God has heard you, you will always have doubt.

So, get ready to kick the doubt out and build your faith up. It is time to build yourself a bulldozer!

The Process

1. Go to the Word and pick out around 5 of your favorite promises. If you have a particular need, then select scriptures that are an answer to your need.
2. Write down each scripture on a card or piece of paper.
3. Find a quiet place and do the following:

   a. Begin by reading the scriptures out loud one at a time.
   b. As you read the scripture, visualize the pictures in them. For example if you are quoting "… whoever says to this mountain be removed…" see that mountain being taken from your path as you quote the passage.
   c. Once you have quoted the scriptures for about five minutes, put them down and spend the next five minutes speaking in tongues.

d. Alternate speaking in tongues and quoting the scriptures. Quoting for five minutes and speaking in tongues for five minutes.

4. As you continue doing this, you will start to feel a stirring inside your spirit. When this happens, now is the time to pray and speak the will of God into your life. Pray the vision through until you begin receiving revelation.

Points to Keep in Mind:

- It is important to keep your mind focused on what you are praying for. Visualize the scriptures and keep that picture in mind when you are speaking in tongues.
- Only pray in English when you feel the build-up in your spirit.
- If you have not done this before, it might take some time before you get the initial breakthrough.

Report Submission

If you are working with a mentor or group leader, submit the following report to them:

1. What scriptures did you pick out?
2. What did you struggle with the most?
3. What have you been believing God for?
4. How long did it take you to feel a build-up on the inside?
5. What are your final feelings and conclusions on this project? What did you get out of it?

About the Author

Born in Bulawayo, Zimbabwe and raised in South Africa, Colette had a zeal to serve the Lord from a young age. Coming from a long line of Christian leaders and having grown up as a pastor's kid, she is no stranger to the realities of ministry. Despite having to endure many hardships such as her parents' divorce, rejection, and poverty, she continues to follow after the Lord passionately. Overcoming these obstacles early in her life has built a foundation of compassion and desire to help others gain victory in their lives.

Since then, the Lord led Colette, with her husband, Craig Toach, to establish *Apostolic Movement International* and *Toach Ministries International*

Apostolic Movement International focuses on training those called to the fivefold ministry whereas *Toach Ministries International* ministers to, covers, supports, and spiritually parents like-minded leaders.

In addition, Colette is a fantastic cook, an amazing mom to not only her four natural children, but to her numerous spiritual children all over the world. Colette is also a renowned author, mentor, trainer, and a woman that has great taste in shoes! The scripture to "be all things to all men" definitely applies to her, and the Lord keeps adding to that list of things each and every day.

How does she do it all? Experience through every book and teaching the life of an apostle firsthand and get the insight into how the call of God can make every aspect of your life an incredible adventure.

Reach Out!

Find out More Here:
www.colette-toach.com

Connect with Colette Toach on Facebook!
www.facebook.com/ColetteToach

Check Colette out on Amazon.com at:
www.amazon.com/author/colettetoach

Connect with Craig and Colette Toach Personally:
www.toach-ministries.com

RECOMMENDATIONS BY THE AUTHOR

Note: All reference of AMI refers to Apostolic Movement International. www.apostolic-movement.com

If you enjoyed this book, I know you will also love the following books and recommendations.

Prophetic Warrior

Book 5 of the Prophetic Field Guide Series

By Colette Toach

Prophet of God, now is the time to face your own limitations and your own bondages and to see what has been holding you back from walking as the warrior that God has called you to be.

How to Hear the Voice of God

By Colette Toach

What you might not realize is that the Lord Jesus is standing right in front of you - wanting this intimacy with you. He is speaking all the time, eager for you to understand what He is saying. This is not something just for prophets or for those that have been walking with the Lord for years. This is something for every believer! This is a relationship Jesus wants with you right now.

Strategies of War

By Colette Toach

No more allowing the enemy to have his way. Take back your land and remove him from your life for good.

Your victory is at hand. So, take hold and allow Colette Toach to guide and teach you the strategy to tearing down the kingdom of darkness

---

Earn a Diploma That Truly Validates Your Call

With over twenty years' experience in full-time ministry, Apostles Craig and Colette Toach know the fire that burns in you to do the work of God.

With a focus on spiritual parenting, mentorship and hands-on training, each school equips you to do the work of God. Consider us boot camp for your fivefold ministry call.

Each course is video based with required report submissions for you to complete after each lesson. Each student is allocated a trainer who marks all reports, follows up with personal ministry and laying on of hands at graduation.

AMI Prophetic School:

www.prophetic-school.com

There is a clear track that the Holy Spirit follows to train up His prophets. Having trained prophets into office all over the world, your calling will find itself in an environment where your prophetic mandate is as important to us as it is to you.

Think: training, impartation and mentorship. By the time you walk the stage at your graduation, you would have done more than just studied for a diploma – you would have embarked on a journey that would have equipped you to fulfill your mandate as a prophet in office.

AMI Pastor Teacher School:

www.pastorteacherschool.com

Everything you wish you knew about doing the work of the ministry. Our student complement consists of pastors, ministry leaders, apostles and various fivefold ministers who crave a deeper reality of the Lord and their calling.

With an emphasis on becoming equipped, each course gears you towards functioning in a leadership capacity. Whether that is behind the pulpit or in a home church setting, you will receive training that by the time you walk the stage, would have already geared you towards apostolic ministry.

AMI Campus:

www.ami-campus.com

Not ready to commit to a lengthy training program? No problem! You are welcome to study independently and pick and choose between prophetic, pastoral, teaching and apostolic courses that tailor fit you right where you are at.

The main difference between our public campus and our other schools is that associates in our campus do not graduate, but rather join a family of like-minded believers. Every associate is supported by qualified pastors and guided through their individual training process. We are here to see your process through!

Contact Information

Check out our wide selection of materials:
www.ami-bookshop.com

Telephone:
+1 (760) 466 - 7679
9am to 5pm California Time, Tuesday - Saturday

E-mail Address:
admin@ami-bookshop.com

Postal Address:

> A.M.I.
> 5663 Balboa Ave #416
> San Diego, CA 92111, USA

Facebook:
http://www.facebook.com/ApostolicMovementInternational

YouTube:
https://www.youtube.com/c/ApostolicMovementInternational

Twitter:
https://twitter.com/apmoveint

Amazon.com:
www.amazon.com/author/colettetoach

AMI Bookshop
It's not **Just Knowledge**, It's **Living Knowledge**

www.ingramcontent.com/pod-product-compliance
Lightning Source LLC
LaVergne TN
LVHW052255070426
835507LV00035B/2915